Peaceful Ocean

Really Relaxing Colouring Book 12

First published in 2015 by Kyle Craig Publishing

Copyright © 2015 Kyle Craig Publishing

Design: Elizabeth James, Julie Anson, Alison McNicol, Shutterstock, Inc.

ISBN: 978-1-78595-080-3

A CIP record for this book is available from the British Library.

A Kyle Craig Publication

www.kyle-craig.com

All Rights Reserved.

No part of this publication may be reproduced, stored in a retrieval system or transmitted by any form or by any means, electronic, recording or otherwise without the prior permission in writing from the publishers.

Unauthorised reproduction of any part of this publication by any means including photocopying is an infringement of copyright.